SHARKS

by Sylvia M. James

Photo Credits:
Front cover: © James D. Watt/Seapics.com; back cover, pp. 6 (top left and right), 12, 13 (top right), 16, 23 (top left), 24 (right): © Marty Snyderman/Waterhouse; pp. 1, 7 (bottom), 28 (top right), 31: © James D. Watt/Watt Wildlife Library; p. 4: © Ray Troll/Seapics.com; pp. 5, 29 (left): © James D. Watt/Animals Animals; p. 6 (bottom): © Ron and Valerie Taylor/Waterhouse; p. 7: (top left): © Deeble & Stone OSF /Animals Animals; p. 7 (top right) © Carl Roessler/Bruce Coleman Inc.; p. 8: © F. Jack Jackson/Bruce Coleman Inc.; p. 9: © George Bernard/Animals Animals; pp. 10 (top), 11, 13 (top left), 14, 18-19: © Ron and Valerie Taylor/Bruce Coleman Inc.; p. 10 (bottom): © Rick Martin/ReefQuest.com; p. 13 (bottom): © Merlen, G. OSF /Animals Animals; p. 15: © James D. Watt/Waterhouse; p. 17: © C & M Fallows/Seapics.com; pp. 20, 24 (left): © Alex Kerstitch/Bruce Coleman Inc.; p. 21: © Jeffrey C. Carrier/Seapics.com; p. 22: © J.R. Williams/Animals Animals; p. 23 (top right): © Dani/Jeske/Animals Animals; p. 23 (bottom): © Bruce Watkins/Animals Animals; pp. 25, 28 (top left): © Norbert Wu/Norbert Wu Productions; pp. 26, 28 (bottom left and right), 30: © Doug Perrine/Seapics.com; p. 27: © Bill Curtsinger/Bill Curtsinger Photography; p. 29 (right): © Tom Brakefield/Bruce Coleman Inc.

Text copyright © 2004 by Sylvia M. James

For information contact:
MONDO Publishing
980 Avenue of the Americas
New York, NY 10018

Visit our web site at http://www.mondopub.com

Printed in China

06 07 08 09 10   10 9 8 7 6 5 4 3 2

ISBN 1-59034-043-4
Designed by Annette Cyr

CONTENTS

What Is a Shark?

Sharks are fish—a very old type of fish.
The first sharks lived about 400 million years ago.

Carcharodon megalodon

The *Carcharodon megalodon*, a huge shark measuring 40 feet (12 m) long, lived 5 to 24 million years ago. It feasted on whales.

Today, there are over 350 different types of sharks.

Sharks live in most of the world's oceans.

Some sharks live alone. Others live in schools, with hundreds of other sharks.

Most sharks live to be about 25 years old, but some live as long as 70 years.

Sharks come in many shapes, sizes, and colors. Some are dangerous, but many are not.

Sawsharks use their long snouts to jab small fish or to dig for other animals in the sand.

Young zebra sharks have dark skin with light stripes and spots. As they get older, their skin becomes lighter with dark spots.

Whale sharks can grow to be 46 feet (14 m) long. They are the biggest fish in the world!

Deep-sea pygmy sharks are only 8 to 10 inches (22 to 25 cm) long.

The wobbegong shark's spots help it blend into the ocean floor.

Hammerhead sharks capture stingrays by pinning them to the ocean floor with their long heads.

Parts of a Shark's Body

All sharks have fins. Some sharks have as many as eight fins.
Each fin has a job to do.

caudal fin

The caudal fin gives the shark power for swimming.

dorsal fins

The dorsal fins keep the shark from rolling upside down when swimming forward.

anal fin
The anal fin keeps the shark from rolling upside down when swimming forward.

pelvic fins
The pelvic fins help the shark swim toward the water's surface.

pectoral fins
The pectoral fins help the shark steer.

A shark's skin is covered with tiny tooth-like scales. The skin protects the shark from anything that gets too close.

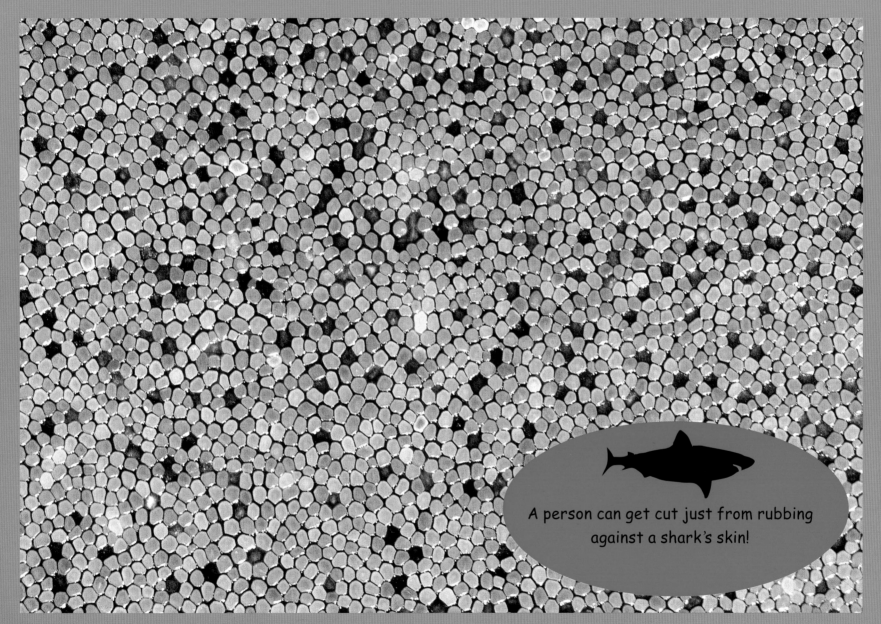

A person can get cut just from rubbing against a shark's skin!

a nurse shark's skin, close-up

A shark's skeleton is made of cartilage. Cartilage is not hard and heavy, like a person's bones; it is light, like plastic. A person's ears are made of cartilage, but a shark's cartilage is much stronger. Cartilage allows a shark to bend, twist, and swim.

shark skeleton

Richard Aiden Martin
ReefQuest.com

All sharks have gills. Sharks use gills to breathe underwater. Gills get oxygen from water. The water goes into the shark's mouth, over the gills, and out the gill slits.

gill slits ————

A shark has between 5 and 15 rows of teeth in its mouth. When a shark loses a tooth, another tooth moves up from the back rows to fill in the space.

A shark loses thousands of teeth in its life.

Different kinds of sharks have different kinds of teeth. The shape of a shark's teeth can tell you what kind of shark it is and how the teeth are used.

A ridged tooth is for tearing meat.

A sharp tooth is for catching food.

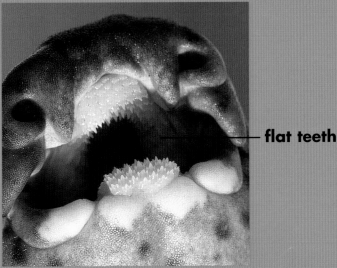
— **flat teeth**

A flat tooth is for crushing shells.

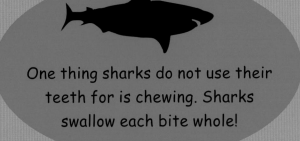
One thing sharks do not use their teeth for is chewing. Sharks swallow each bite whole!

13

What Sharks Eat

All sharks are meat eaters.

a grey-reef-shark feeding frenzy

Some sharks eat very small food. The whale shark eats plankton.

Most plankton are too small to see without a microscope!

a whale shark eating plankton

Other sharks eat small and medium-sized food from the ocean floor. Zebra sharks eat crab, shrimp, and small fish.

Some sharks will eat anything they can fit inside their mouths! Tiger sharks sometimes even eat tin cans and license plates!

zebra shark

Some sharks hunt for larger prey. The great white shark eats seals, sea lions, dolphins, whales, squid, turtles, and even other sharks.

After a big meal, a shark might not eat for two or three days.

great white shark

Many sharks are good hunters. To catch prey, sharks use their senses.

HEARING: Some sharks can hear their prey moving in the water from more than a half mile (.8 km) away.

SMELL: Sharks can smell a single drop of blood in a million drops of water!

SIGHT: Sharks can see well in the dark.

TASTE:

Sharks use taste buds to tell if their prey does not taste good. A bad taste means the prey might be poisonous!

TOUCH: Sharks have a row of holes along the sides of their bodies. There are little hairs inside the holes. The hairs let them feel movement as prey swims by.

hark Pups

Baby sharks are called pups. There are two different ways sharks have pups. Some types of sharks lay eggs. Other types of sharks give birth.

newly hatched swell shark and empty egg cases

Unlike the eggs of most fish, a shark's eggs are fertilized while they are still inside the female.

two nurse sharks mating

Some egg-laying sharks lay their eggs in shallow water.
The shallow water will have food for the new pups when they hatch.

A shark egg is protected by an egg case. Egg cases start out soft, but soon get hard. They come in different shapes that help protect the pups inside.

Horn shark and Port Jackson shark egg cases are shaped like screws and can wedge into rocks and sand.

A swell shark egg case has hooks on one end to grab onto seaweed. This camouflages the egg case.

When a pup hatches, it looks like a tiny adult shark. It has a full set of teeth. The pup can swim and hunt. The pup is ready to take care of itself as soon as it hatches.

horn shark pup

adult horn shark

Some sharks take more than a year to hatch.

Most types of sharks do not hatch from eggs. The pups grow inside the mother. The mother's body gives them protection and food.

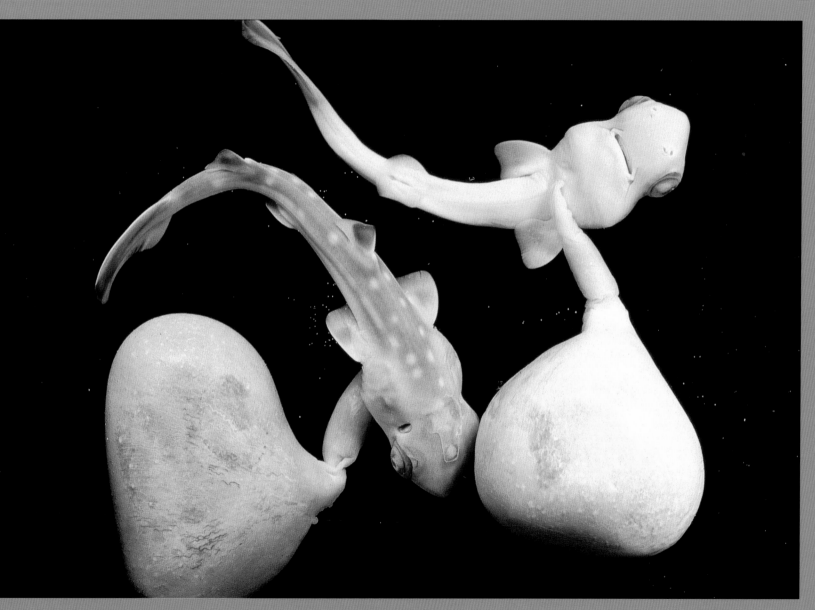

This is what baby dogfish sharks look like inside the mother shark.

When the pups get big enough, they are born. Some pups are six inches (15 cm) long when born. Others can be two feet (60 cm) long. All pups are born with a full set of teeth and are ready to hunt.

live birth of a lemon shark pup

Some sharks give birth to hundreds of pups at one time. Others give birth to just one or two.

Sharks and People

People hunt so many sharks that some types may become extinct.

Fishermen kill between 30 million and 100 million sharks a year. Why?

People eat sharks. People use sharks to make things like jewelry and boots. People think sharks make fishing difficult.

shark meat

shark tooth necklace

sharkskin boots

shark fin soup

Many people are afraid of sharks. Sharks attack a small number of people each year. Those attacks usually take place because the shark thinks the person is a sea creature. Only a few kinds of sharks are dangerous to humans.

tiger shark

great white shark

In the year 2000, only 79 people were attacked by sharks. Most of the attacks were by great white and tiger sharks.

Many people are surprised to learn that sharks can help people. Since sharks do not get sick very often, scientists study them to learn how people can stay healthy, too.

We can learn from sharks. People need to protect sharks. They are an important part of life in the ocean!

Glossary

cartilage   the soft flexible tissue found in your ears and on the tip of your nose; sharks have skeletons made of cartilage

egg case   a tough, leathery covering that protects a shark's egg

extinct   having no individuals of a species left alive

gills   feathery structures on a fish that are behind the gill slits and that remove oxygen from the water so that the fish can breathe

gill slits   the openings on the head of a fish that connect to the gills

oxygen   the part of air and water that all animals need to breathe to survive

plankton   tiny plants and animals that float and drift in the ocean

prey   any animal that is hunted by another animal for food